MW01709495

Lori!

Thank You for being part of this honorable + noble profession and the Artful Asking Success Club!

Invest in JOY!

Nancy

(and Lori, too!)

Withism's From Lori: Boldness, Clarity & Wisdom for Fundraising Professionals Making a Difference

By Lori L. Jacobwith

WITHISM'S FROM LORI

Boldness, clarity and wisdom for fundraising professionals making a difference.

A COLLECTION OF BLOG POSTS

volume 1 Spring 2012

LoriJacobwith.com
Where your mission meets its match.

Withism's from Lori:
Boldness, Clarity & Wisdom for Fundraising Professionals

ISBN 978-0-578-10294-8

Table of Contents

Introduction

I truly believe fundraising can be accomplished with ease and genuine joy. My life's passion is creating environments where ease is present and causes extraordinary results. I've spent my career working with board members, staff and whole organizations to take the fear and anxiety out of raising money.

It was this belief that led me to start my blog, **Withism's from Lori: Boldness clarity & wisdom for fundraising professionals making a difference**. Every week I spend some time to provide insights and coaching, go on a few rants, and share as much as I can about what works and how you can succeed when it comes to fundraising.

With posts that include tips on storytelling, how to share you mission powerfully, and suggestions on how to engage your board my blog has become an invaluable resource, or so readers tell me. Because of the encouragement I've gotten from readers and the requests that inundate by inbox asking about specific posts, I decided to create this book, *Withism's from Lori: Boldness, Clarity & Wisdom for Fundraising Professionals Making a Difference.*

This book represents the thirty most popular, most commented on posts from the first four years of my blog now in one easy-to-read place. In here you'll find "Ten Ways to Increase Your Donor Retention," "Staying Sane with Social Media," "Talking about Money So People Want to Give," and much more.

When you read these pages I hope you come away inspired and encouraged to tackle your biggest goals. Even more than that, I hope this book represents the passion and joy I feel for my work and the work you, as fundraisers, do for the organizations we love.

Thank you so much for reading!

Lori L. Jacobwith

Blessing or Curse: Board Members & Fund Development

An Excerpt From my 'Nine Steps to A Successful Fundraising Campaign' e-book

I believe successful development efforts have all board members participating in fund development in some capacity and I don't just mean the "Hey, you're doing a great job" cheerleading role.

Being a board member is not just an honor to bestow on people who show up at meetings. Board seats are critical to the financial success of your organization.

I can just feel some people squirming as I write this. I can read your mind, too: "But Lori, you don't know my organization—my board can't/won't agree to that!"

Are you sure?

The reality is, without FULL board participation and a clear understanding of your financial needs, your work as an organization is far more difficult.

How do you get the board to support your fund development work? Start with an expectation and accountability discussion. When the board members started their term of service, were they told directly that being a part of fund development is expected of them? Was their role clearly defined? And do you have one or more advocates on your board who will strongly support your efforts to get all the board members, well, "on board"?

Here's what I mean: In the interview process, it's critical that both fundraising (the raising of assets) and fund development (raising of visibility and deepening engagement) activities be thoroughly discussed and outlined. New board members must know beyond any doubt that they will be included in some of the "doing" as well as the giving.

A frequent frustration I bump into is that the development staff doesn't know—because they haven't discussed it or created a plan around it—what they want from the board, so the board is left to figure it out on their own. It's as if you want me to know how to scuba dive because I love being in the water, but no one ever takes the time to teach me to do it.

Participation doesn't mean the board members must directly ask for financial contributions. Here's a short list of things that a board member or key volunteer can do to assist your organization in maintaining deep, connected relationships with donors, and they do not ever have to ask someone else for a financial contribution:

- Make phone calls to donors to thank them for their recent contribution.

- Invite donors, volunteers, community members, family, friends, colleagues, and others to your events, including the "get to know us" type of events that are free.

- Take a current or former donor to coffee to thank them for their recent gift. Obviously it's not practical to take every donor out; set a minimum donation goal for this type of activity.

- Make an introduction to the community affairs person at their workplace.

- Give a heartfelt—but short—speech at their church or civic group to invite interest in your organization.

This is only a short list of the many ways board members can actively participate in fund development activities. Whatever role they play, staff and board must be clear and specific about expectations. Then staff assists by providing data so that board members can hold themselves accountable. Discussion of these metrics may cause great strides in your keeping donors connected and engaged.

Let me know what other ways your organization uses board members in fund development efforts.

Originally posted February 24, 2010

Nine Steps for Successful Fundraising Campaigns

Is your organization READY to change course?

I regularly receive invitations from people who are hunting for "the thing" or "the person" who will help their nonprofit catapult their fundraising to a whole new stratosphere. The two real-life* examples I have to share are, unfortunately, more of the norm than the exception. These are examples of when the "desire doesn't match the readiness."

Organization A: Working hard to keep rivers & lakes protected, wants to enhance their fundraising quickly and get the board more involved with reaching out to others. One .5 staff person. Annual budget of nearly $250,000.

- When I asked if 100% of the board makes a financial contribution to the organization they said NO.
- When I asked how much they needed to raise from the community each year. They weren't sure.

- When I asked to attend a board meeting to learn more about their fundraising goals they explained that they don't discuss those issues at board meetings so, NO.

Readiness factor on my 9 point scale: 0

Organization B: With a revolutionary approach to educating and assimilating people with disabilities into the community, they have start-up grant funds from one funder to get things rolling. Because they have enough to open their doors, they decided to "wait" to talk about fundraising goals and set a plan for how to invite the community to support their work until they fill the classroom with students.

When I asked if we could create an action plan to incorporate the areas of interest of board members into raising awareness about their program and include some training on how to talk about "the money" they said, NO not yet. We are not ready for that.
Readiness factor on my 9 point scale: 0

My 2009 eBook *Nine Steps for Successful Fundraising Campaigns* was written to help organizations flesh out their readiness to raise more dollars. It's a list of what I look for when I'm invited to "help" or work with an organization. I still use it to this day. You can download the eBook on my website, but let me recap it with a different slant, turning the steps into questions for your team to ponder:

1. Does your organization have at least one key volunteer and/or staff member who will make sure fundraising happens all year long? (*Board Chair, CEO, Executive Director, Pastor, Rabbi*)

2. After you raise some additional funds, will you add staff (e.g. a development director, development

associate) to support and manage the fundraising tasks?

3. Does your board make a financial contribution to the organization? And do they understand their role is to help raise awareness & invite support of the organization?

4. About the money: Does your team, including your staff and board, understand how much money you have to raise from the community this year? Do you have a specific timeline that creates a sense of urgency?

5. Do you share stories of the people you serve to create an emotional connection – making it personal for people to participate?

6. Does your organization communicate regularly, via multi-channel methods of communication to keep donors and interested parties informed and engaged?

7. Does your organization keep your vision for growth and your annual fundraising goal visible in print, in person at meetings, on your website, in your newsletter & emails to encourage widespread participation?

8. Throughout the year does your organization invite supporters to do very specific things with a deadline for doing them?

9. Do you have a donor data management system (preferably web-based) to allow others to assist with tracking donor contacts and gifts? Something more sophisticated than an Excel spreadsheet?

**Real-life examples: details have been changed to the keep these organizations anonymous.*

Originally published February 29, 2011

Four Words to Describe a Great Fundraiser

They might surprise you

On a recent phone call with my colleague and friend Chad Brown, he used these four words to describe a great development officer, especially a great major gifts officer. And Chad would know, he's been doing major gifts work for years and is currently a Vice President Consultant, Major Gifts Officer with the Greater Twin Cities United Way in Minneapolis, MN.

Confidante. Someone who listens with discretion. It's important when talking with people about money that information learned be held close to the vest due to all the important and private things that may be shared.

CEO. The person with the vision who creates an amazing plan. In this case it's the annual development plan. This is the take-charge attitude. Development officers exhibiting CEO-type behavior motivate others to help them reach the agency fundraising goals.

Entrepreneur. Great development officers are self-motivated with a drive for results. They don't need someone looking over their shoulder to meet their goals and often exceed by using new, outside the box strategies.

Ringmaster. This one is really important. They get in the limelight when it's important to do so. And then they take themselves out of the limelight to shine the light on others: donors, staff & volunteers.

As Chad explained to me, awesome development officers are all of these at some point in their day. And sometimes they are all of these in the same meeting. Which are you today?

Originally posted March 10, 2010

Seven Steps for Making Better Donor Thank you Calls

Meaningful, authentic calls have more impact

Last week I shared some resources you can use in planning the most effective way to thank and engage your donors. As I promised, here are my recommendations for donor thank you calls.

First, it's important that making these calls not just become a task that someone crosses off their "to do" list. The call has to be meaningful and authentic to really make an impact, whether it's a voice-to-voice conversation or a voice mail message.

You can use this outline to help make the thank you calls made by your staff, board members, or community volunteers more meaningful.

1. Use the person's name. I know, really we have to tell our callers that? Don't they already know? You'd be surprised what happens when your callers do this at home, alone. I often suggest doing calls like these in a group at a board meeting, development committee meeting or at a special "thank-a-thon" event.

2. Identify the callers' relationship to your organization: board member, former board, long-time volunteer.

3. Say something about the recent gift: size, frequency, etc. Have this caller KNOW something REAL about the donor such as when they started giving, how long they've given.

4. Keep voice mail messages warm and short.

5. If it's a voice-to-voice call, indicate early in the call that this is a call to say thank you. Nothing more.

6. If there is a willingness to talk for a moment have the caller tell something about a real person who has received services and how their life is different or better because of the work your organization does. One or two sentences is all.

7. OR if there is a willingness to talk for a moment ask a question about why the donor gave, or why they started giving? An open-ended question that allows the caller to learn something new about this donor is invaluable.

Originally posted April 7, 2010

One of the Best eNewsletters I've Seen in Awhile

Whether fundraising or informing, communication is key

Last week I received the enewsletter on the next page. Honestly, I've not yet given to this organization but I found this message compelling and it got me to take action, more than once. I visited their website, read articles, learned some new things, and felt connected. Do your email newsletters do that?

Five tips for creating a great enewsletter:

1. **Personalize.** If Amazon.com can say "Hello Lori" every time I return to their site, the technology is there to personalize messages to supporters or those you hope become your supporters.

2. **Emotional connection.** There was a touching story about real people and it taught me some things about what the Minnesota Medical Foundation does.

3. Helpful information. There were no strings attached to the three different bits of helpful information like Organizing for Tax-Time Success Year-Round. The information was found by clicking on the link to "read more" which brought me directly to their website. Newsletters can and should drive traffic to your constantly updated website.

4. Easy to give. The Donate Now button was easy to find with a compelling tag line: "You can make a difference today."

5. **Easy to contact.** There was a whole section of more helpful links and information should I choose to become a donor: Gift Calculator, Meet Our Donors, Legal Essentials, and Contact Us.

The overall look of this message was: colorful, inviting, easy to read, and compelled me to click/take action, plus I was appreciative that I learned new information. The message seemed to say: "You are important to us." How does your communication measure up?

Originally posted April 22, 2010

You Can Say a lot in Six Words

Fundraising stories don't have to be long or boring

A year or so ago I heard a story on public radio about a book called *Not Quite What I Was Planning*. It's a paperback book of six-word memoirs written by people from all across the country. It's grown into a huge deal. You can check out the website from Smith Magazine for more details.

The radio story really struck a chord for me because I love the idea of telling a lot with so few words. Now, I often have board members and staff create short stories like these in the workshops and fundraising action planning sessions I deliver. I've found that people are amazed what can be learned from such a small number of words.

Six-word stories can be used as a headline in a newsletter article, in the subject line for an email you really want read, as the first line of a direct mail letter, on websites, you name it. And yes, less really is more.

Last summer at a Volunteers of America conference in Denver, Jim White from the Colorado affiliate office showed me his collection of six-word stories. Here is one of them:

If you remember that when people read something about your organization you want them to want to know MORE. . . then these stories are perfect and packed with lots of emotional connection for readers.

I encourage organizations to create a list of six-word stories as a team building exercise at a planning meeting or board meeting. You'll be amazed at how creative your team can be.

Here are a few more to get your creative juices going

First Ernest Hemingway's famous story: For sale. Baby shoes. Never worn.

From Life House in Duluth, MN an awesome organization serving homeless teens: Homeless doesn't have to be hopeless.

From the Ely, MN winter festival: Shhhh! Winter in Ely is fabulous!

My own: Creates compelling stories to raise millions.

What's your six-word story that will cause people to want to learn more about you? Let me know!

Originally posted April 28, 2010

Ten Ways to Increase Your Donor Retention

Simple tips to help you stand out from the crowd of fundraisers

I read a post from Seth Godin on Monday that got me thinking about how donors are treated and why they leave. Here's the post, "No New Customers"

> *"What if a rift in the time-space continuum changed the universe and it was suddenly impossible to get new customers, new readers, new donors, or new viewers?*
>
> *How would that change what you do all day and how you spend your money and what you measure?*
>
> *What if you tried acting that way now?"*

So really, what might your organization do differently if you knew for certain the donors you have are the only ones you are ever going to have?

Here's a list of things that make a difference in donor retention. These are tasks for both board and staff. What would you add to it?

1. Occasionally make a phone call to learn more about them or thank them.
2. Invite financial supporters in small groups to meet with your CEO in an intimate setting to see or participate in something special.
3. Listen. Learn more about them than they learn about you.
4. Involve them in ways they have mentioned that matter to them.
5. Send less email and spend more quality time in person.
6. Notice them and talk with them at events.
7. Personalize appeals so they know their gift matters.
8. Let them know about successes and concerns.
9. Treat them like insiders.
10. Ask for their advice and act on it.

The truth is it takes time to conduct your day so that it is this donor-focused. The reward is you build a deeper relationship that lasts. And you'll stand out from the crowd of organizations doing things the same old way allowing hundreds of donors to slip away each year.

What are you committed to? Keeping your supporters or losing them?

Originally posted May 5, 2010

Yours for the Asking

Information from Reynold Levy's guide to fundraising & management

Does your organization have enough money to do what you want to do? To serve as many people as need your services? As Reynold Levy says in one of my favorite fundraising books, *Yours For the Asking*:

> *"The contribution of this nation's Third Sector to meeting... twenty-first-century challenges is constrained by a lack of resources. Acquiring them with a greater sense of urgency, of competency and of creativity is a critical task. It can be accomplished, but only if the chief executive becomes personally engaged and catalyzes volunteers and professional staff with vision and by example."*

I believe, as Reynold does, that the Chief Executive must both lead the charge by example but also engage a group of volunteers and key staff to help raise the funds needed to do the work.

In my work with social profit organizations of all shapes and sizes, I'm troubled that it's rare that I find a chief executive who is willing to dive in and make development efforts a major part of their focus.

The rule of thumb for the successful CEOs I encounter is that about 50% of their time is spent tending donor relationships or inviting financial support.

Reynold says: "Put simply, fundraising is nothing more than salesmanship. It's persuasiveness at work. It's a performing art." And he should know, as CEO of the Lincoln Center for Performing Arts he's raised millions. His book is an easy to follow guidebook/roadmap for the different arenas of development: events, individual solicitation, board engagement, appeals, and on. I love this book and give it as a gift, often.

I find Reynold's no-nonsense style to be refreshing and exciting. He is someone who loves to provide an opportunity to others to be their greatest selves by supporting the organizations he's worked for.

Reynold understands that "the ask" is not about him. And he understands that he must know his organization's financial supporters intimately for them to feel engaged and "insider" enough to give more of their advice, time and dollars. He makes sure donors to his organization feel "seen" and therefore feel special.

So I ask you:
What amount of time have you spent, today, to connect with a donor?

- Who did you thank for their gift?
- Who did you invite to make a gift?
- Who did you contact to provide some feedback about

how a recent gift was put to good use?

- Where did you deepen a connection and cause someone to feel special for supporting your organization?

- Do you know the faces & names of your top 25 or 30 or even 100 supporters?

- Do those supporters know that they are special to your organization for more than just their annual check?

Originally posted on May 26, 2010

What Happened to Voice-to-Voice Communication?

Staying connected, really connected should be personal sometimes

I've got an issue that's been on my mind for a while. With the explosion of social media it appears that we have forgotten that voice to voice or in-person communication is the most personal way to connect with our family, friends, donors, and volunteers.

I was recently visiting a friend and as she was sitting in the living room talking with me she sent her son a text IN THE NEXT ROOM. For me, that's taking this whole social media thing a bit too far.

I happen to love social media. I use Twitter and Facebook regularly. I post videos on YouTube. I send out monthly eNewseltters and I often read and comment on postings on the web. This isn't a slam on social media. I believe it has value, it's fun and I've gotten to know some amazing people from around the world thanks to social media.

This is my plea for some sanity around using more personal methods of communication with the most cherished people in our lives. And if you are in the social profit sector that means your financial supporters and volunteers.

A few months ago, after I had sent out my monthly eNewsletter I received an email reply from Gary asking me a question. I did what I like to do: I picked up the phone and called Gary, whom I'd met once, to thank him for reading my newsletter and proceeded to answer the question. The response I got was: "Oh, you're calling me! I didn't want to bother you. I just wanted a quick answer on email."

I explained that the phone call was much faster and it wasn't a bother. I made an effort to explain that it felt more personal to me to actually make the call. I attempted to make sure Gary knew that his question was important to me. I'm still not sure he'd recovered by the end of the call.

I'm concerned the trend is to rely on email and eNewsletters to lure ourselves into thinking we are staying in touch with people in a compelling and personal way.

I receive more than 100 emails most days. Some of which are very impersonal and most days the total unread messages can be overwhelming.

While I don't advocate phoning every donor monthly, an annual, meaningful phone call from the right person, has huge value. The side benefit is the person knows for just a minute or two that they are special to your organization. And a face-to-face interaction – well that packs an ever more powerful punch for building a deeper relationship.

I believe there is still room for personal communication in our work and in our lives. Live or voice mail. It's still good. Warm, authentic messages to say hello, thank you or ask for some quick advice from a long-time donor.

My request: If I phone you, please, please don't send me an email reply. Just pick up the phone and let's talk, voice to voice, for a minute or five to get our "thing" handled or scheduled and then move on with our day.

Whew, I feel better!

Originally posted June 23, 2010

Measuring Your Success with Major Gifts

It's not all about the fundraising dollars

I'm often asked how to rate the effectiveness of a major gifts officer. . . other than the obvious measure: dollars in. While bringing in gifts is important, especially for a new major gifts officer, I don't feel it is the only measure of effectiveness.

At www.majorgivingnow.org I found a helpful article by Richard K. Dupree: "Measuring Performance – A Station Manger's Guide to Evaluating Major Gifts Officers."

Although this article is based on staff in public broadcasting I believe the tool shared is very helpful in measuring the effectiveness of any major gifts officer.

This is also a great tool to use to measure the first 90 days of employment as well as annually.

The thing I like the best about this tool is that it weights all four areas equally. Creating an environment for both long and short-term effectiveness.

Here's a recap of the article and the four areas to measure:

1. **Dollar goal** – while important, Dupree believes this is the least important of the four measures. I agree that even first-year major gifts officers should be presented with a defined dollar goal of cash/cash pledges and deferred gifts. By equally weighting this area with the other four the system builds in long-term success as well as rewards for short-term wins.

2. **Proposals/Asks** – Set a goal for the minimum number of proposals or actual asks to be generated each year. To guard against a staffer sending out a large number of unfunded proposals or asking too early, the "hit rate" is measured in section four.

3. **Contacts** – This is a key area to measure. A pre-determined number of annual contacts should be established with the highest percentage of these being face-to-face.

4. **Overall Quality of Work** – There are five aspects to measure. Each is given the same weight and they build on the three previous measures.

    - Hit rate: Simply measure the ratio of yeses to no's in the proposals submitted or asks made.

    - Prospecting: Pre-determine the number of visits at the start of the fiscal year. This is critical in keeping the pipeline filled and the acquisition rate growing.

	Points
• **Dollar goal (cash & pledges)**	**25**
• **Proposals submitted**	**25**
• **Contacts**	**25**
• **Quality of Work**	**25**
A. "Hit Rate"	*5*
B. Prospecting	*5*
C. Cultivations	*5*
D. Use of management/leadership	*5*
E. Budget management	*5*
	100

- Cultivations: These are meetings with individuals who are not new to the organization and may be much closer to making or accepting a proposal for a major gift. These visits are also important in maintaining an appropriate retention rate with existing donors.

- Use of management/leadership: This is a great way to encourage and remind major gifts officers that management and board leadership can and should be involved in key solicitations.

- Budget management: Being responsible for their own costs associated with bringing in a major gift can be a great safeguard against incurring expenses that may not be necessary.

The system is based on 100 points and Dupree says a score of 80 or higher would illustrate above-standard performance. The full article is listed in the Resources section of LoriJacobwith.com. It's a very thorough discussion of these measures and has a link to download the Word document too.

Originally posted July 14, 2010

It's Logical: More Askers = More Money

Suggestions from Andy Robinson about fundraising

A few weeks ago I listened to a terrific webinar sponsored by the Minnesota Council of Nonprofits with guest speaker Andy Robinson. If you've not heard of him, he's a great guy who provides consulting and coaching for grassroots organizations.

Why I loved the session from Andy is that he shared a step-by-step common sense approach to increasing the numbers of "askers" on your development team. No they aren't board members, though they could be. They are your staff. In fact ALL of your staff.

Andy says in many organizations "what is usually lacking is enough people to do the asking." He then went on to share a case study about Toxics Action that shuts down for two weeks a year and has ALL staff engage in their major gifts solicitations. Face to face asks are made by everyone from the admin staff to the program manager. When people are hired they are told: everyone is a fundraiser here.

No one is exempt. We'll teach you how to do it. And they do.

While your organization may or may not be able to devote the kind of focus Toxics Action does, this model is adaptable to different size staffs and different kinds of organizations.

The reality is donors will give five to ten times more in person than they will give via mail. So at Toxics Action they train their staff to go out and meet with donors. This kind of fundraising is like conducting your own market research. You get to ask donors questions face-to-face and really learn more about why they give.

Andy referred to this model as the Ambassador model. What I believe, as does Andy, is that "more money exists out there...it's just hidden from your view."

What I learned from Andy:
To be successful raising money from individual you need four things:

- A strong case.
- A list of prospective donors.
- People to do the asking.
- A system in place to track data, money, and donor recognition.

What can make a difference in increasing your fundraising dollars?

- Set up time to train everyone in what the current objections might be to making a larger gift right now.
- Allow people time to get comfortable answering those objections with thoughtful answers and comments.

- Practice. Practice. Practice.
- Everyone participates.

Here's part of the compelling story Andy shared:

> *After five years of building their major gifts program, Toxics Action now raises $110,000 per year — one-quarter of its annual budget — from individual major gifts of at least $250. Using the time and talents of eight staff members, only one of whom is a full-time fundraiser, the organization conducts 250 to 300 donor visits each year in homes spread across six states.*

In an article you can download from the Grassroots Fundraising Journal (www.grassrootsfundraising.org), Andy shares in detail about the Toxic Actions story and shares a powerful example of how a married couple increased their gift from $45 to $1500 using this model.

Originally posted August 4, 2010

Feeling Good is What Nonprofits Sell

I had the great honor to spend a day with Seth Godin last week. At the event I asked a question about how to get board members and entrenched staff to really dive into fundraising.

I was looking for advice on how to move some of my clients and members outside their comfort zone to engage others in giving money.

My paraphrasing of Seth's answer:

> *"Many CEOs of social profit organizations don't really know how to give and therefore struggle with the ask. The reality is some CEOs don't understand what it means to have their work be art and truly give. Transactions pull people apart. Gifts pull people together. What may hold a staff back is the inability to relate authentically to the person who gets asked for money every day. The act of giving adds meaning to our work. And many social profit CEOs don't often GIVE the investor or potential investor a way to feel good."*

It's our job to allow those we are inviting to support our work to "feel" something. And what social profit organizations really sell is the ability for their supporters and their investors to feel good about giving and about the work being done.

The way we can give that experience is through authentic conversations that tell true stories about the good work being done and the real people being served. Communicating in a way that causes people to feel something is, I believe, the most important part of the asking process.

What worries me, and what Seth Godin mentioned in a story he shared, is that often people in the social sector are too worried about the pain of others knowing their finances, or their daily struggle or they don't want to deal with the pain of telling the truth in some way.

This prevents them from sharing their compelling story. It gets glossed over with a "we are doing fine" comment that causes the listener to feel absolutely nothing. Or, worst-case scenario, it causes them to feel they are not needed.

I encourage you to embrace Seth's list of ways to embrace the new American Dream (from page 33 of his newest bestselling book *Linchpin*) and allow your organization and the people you serve to be rewarded.

I invite you to:

- Be remarkable
- Be generous
- Create art – (the act of taking personal responsibility, challenging the status quo, and changing people)
- Make judgment calls
- Connect people and ideas
- Be accessible

. . . then see what kind of support shows up for your organization.

Originally posted September 1, 2010

Three Philanthropists Tell the Truth

Advice for fundraisers from donors

Do you know what the people who give you money want from you in return for their financial gift? For some it's a simple thank you note. For others it's to know their gift has lasting impact. For others, well, we don't know unless we ask them.

So I did.

During one of my webinars for members I asked three philanthropists who have collectively given more than $100 million to social profit organizations some questions about why they give, why they stop giving, and what advice they have for development staff. We had two men and one woman. Ages ranged from 40s to 70s. Here is what they had to say:

What causes you to make a financial gift?

- Emotion
- Personal connection

Why stop supporting an organization?

- Concerns about executive or board leadership
- Feel taken for granted and under appreciated
- Don't feel ongoing personal connection
- Individual giving priorities have changed
- Wasn't really connected to the mission in the first place, but rather gave initially because a friend was involved

How do you decide what size gift to make?

- The level of passion I have causes me to stretch
- Personal involvement
- The need has been articulated clearly ($__________ will do __________)
- The need and cost associated with that need are clear

Pitfalls of fundraisers

- They don't listen. They only go on about their organization. They need to listen and ask questions to learn about my priorities, passion and interests

Overall advice

- Make sure NEED has been explained fully
- Do homework, personalize and customize approach
- Create passion & find out what I'm passionate about
- Provide tangible opportunities for a donor to fill a need
- Try different approaches

- Keep good donor records

- Know that not everyone is a fit or cares about your mission, even after you explain it to them. Be okay with letting them go but don't forget to ask if they know someone who would be interested

- Match the ASKER to the DONOR (especially in regards to larger gifts over $1k). The ASKER should have some sort of relationship with the DONOR and always have them accompanied by staff or board member who can speak to the mission and organization details.

Their answers may not surprise you. But will they cause YOU to take action and find out what YOUR supporters are thinking? I hope so.

Originally posted September 29, 2010

Two Powerful Words

Increase your fundraising by eliminating these words

I believe it is one thing, and one thing only, that cause success in life. Communication.

In addition to the actions we take each day to raise funds, recruit board members, make thank you calls to donors, and so on, the words we choose when we speak have a significant effect on the outcome.

Most of us have heard this definition of insanity: Doing the same thing over and over again and expecting different results.

When I really, truly heard that statement it was like a thunderbolt. It dawned on me: **I actually have to think and speak differently to get different results.**

Here's a tip: Old patterns are powerful. They have strong grip on you. In order to shift outcomes, identify bite-sized opportunities for shifting behavior. You make communication choices all day long. And I find most people's choices are less than inspiring. Here's an example:

Utilitarian: We need your help. Please give us money.
Inspiring: It took just $80 to help Tony, age 19, get his GED this year because of supporters like you. Our goal is to serve 100 more Tonys this year from our waiting list of 500. Will you invest in a few more Tonys this year?

To change your story and your outcomes you have to change the words you use. That's how better results show up. There are two words I believe can be destructive and stop progress.

"Can't" is a destructive little word

How many times a day do you say or hear the word "can't?" Pay attention for a day and see what you find – in yourself and in those around you. You may be surprised at the power this little word is wielding over your life.

Eliminate this word!

When I'm giving training strategy sessions or meeting with a client, I often count how many times I hear the word "can't" coming from the team. They don't know why I'm putting those marks on the whiteboard, but when I tell them I've captured the number of times they used the word "can't" they're usually shocked at the reality right in front of them. Sometimes I hear "can't" so often I'm unable to keep up with the tally.

I invite you to take a look at how many times you can use words OTHER than "can't". Looking at the day or the situation without negatives – allows it to be a pure, unfettered opportunity.

"Try" avoids commitment to success

Quote from Jedi Master Yoda, from "Star-Wars": **Do, or do not. There is no try.**

"Try" is a cop out. If you want to limit your responsibility and waffle on a commitment use "try".

Here are some examples:

- I'll "try" to get that done (But if I don't finish at least I tried).
- I'll "try" to make the deadline (When I miss it you can't be mad, I tried).
- I'll "try" to change my behavior (I may not, but I'll tell you I'm trying in order to buy time and make myself feel better).

"Try" avoids a commitment to success.

I've noticed for some, commitments have become something we keep if they are convenient for us. We'll try – but do we feel anything close to failure if we don't deliver on that commitment?

NEWS FLASH: People will pay good money for the secret to getting things done. I'll give you the secret for free. Want to get things done? Do them! Don't just try.

I share the Yoda quote often when I speak and recently I shared it at a conference in Wisconsin. The conference host sat in on my session. She runs a statewide organization and is very accomplished and successful.

Deborah sent me a thank you email after the conference and said:

> *"The most powerful changes are taking place here in our office since we adopted the Do or Do not strategy." She said, "TRY is outlawed here and we are having so much more fun and accomplishing so much more! It's an invaluable lesson. Thank you!"*

My recommendation? Take these changes on in bite-sized pieces that work for you. You're not going to feel happy or at peace by trying to adhere to a strict new set of goals or ideals – mine or anyone else's.

Fun fact: At 211 degrees water is hot. Very hot. But at 212 degrees it boils! And with boiling water comes steam and steam can power a locomotive. . . big things can happen with a tiny difference. Make a tiny difference today and create big results.

Originally posted October 20, 2010

Mission Moments

Creating an army of ambassadors

What if you could have a team or an army of people who talk about your organization every day? People who were proud to share stories about the impact of the life-changing work being done at your organization? Telling stories so compelling people who hear them want to take action and give their time or financial support?

It's a simple but powerful tool I often recommend to organizations I work with, begin a practice of holding a "mission moment" at meetings and gatherings with staff and board.

I define a "mission moment" as any example of how your organization is making an impact. It's an example about a real person, family, or human situation.

- It can be a board member telling how they felt to participate at your recent fundraising event.

- It can be a staff person talking about the family that got turned away that day.
- It can be a volunteer saying thank you for allowing them to "work" with your organization.

Mission moments are short, inspirational examples of your work that put a face on what you do. They are stories and examples that can be repeated by others because they are not too long. They are inspiring and often give visibility to something you'd like to do more of but due to limited resources you simply can't do all that you'd like.

I recently heard a mission moment about Neal, a young man with Down Syndrome who, after a great deal of support in a residential housing environment, made a toast at his brother's wedding — to a room of 200 people! Making a toast in front of lots of people can scare many of us, but the work done at this organization made it possible for Neal to feel great, be prepared, and able to share in a special family event. The telling of the story of his toast was a memorable moment for Neal and for the organization that provides him ongoing care and support.

The story was shared in such a way that listeners wanted to learn more about how to help. That's what I call a powerful mission moment.

So, how to begin?

1. Make time at each staff, board, and committee meeting. Ask for someone to share an example of a "mission moment." (You may have to be the first example to show people how to do it.)

2. Just one “mission moment” shared at each meeting is plenty.

3. Rotate who shares.

4. Keep the sharing to literally a minute or two at the most.

5. No rules about what the mission moment is about.

6. Get people talking and connecting about real people and real feelings.

This is also a great activity to kick off a one-on-one donor visit. Ask THEM if they have an example of a mission moment for why they support your organization. OR you share a short example of your work as a mission moment to connect the donor to something fresh and new about your organization.

The moments shared do not always have to have a happy ending. But they DO always have to cause people to feel something.

Start today. It will change things. I promise. And you WILL build an army of people who share powerful stories about your organization.

Originally posted January 12, 2011

Practicing the Ask

This week I had the honor of co-delivering a mini-workshop about how to deliver a powerful and successful 2, 5, or 10 minute presentation to a prospective funder with colleague and friend, Barbara Haley, from SteppsUp.

Our task was to help the nonprofit organizations in the Red Wing, Minnesota area get ready for their annual United Way presentations next month.

We provided some reminders and some Do's and Don'ts about asking for money in person. Then, using Flip cameras, we videotaped as many of the speakers as possible while they practiced their presentations. Videotaping is a really great way to see what habits you have that you may want to change.

And as we all know, practice makes perfect.

Here is some feedback we gave to those practicing their presentations:

State the dollar amount for the funding request multiple times.

Don't just say it once, all in a rush at the end of the presentation. Be comfortable conveying what your organization will do with the gift. In fact, starting off with a sentence like: "I'm here today to provide you with a compelling reason to fund our $10,000 grant proposal" is a great idea.

Talk about the impact of your work more than the features of your programs.

Funders are not as interested in the fact that you have 12 volunteers working in the crisis phone center each day. What they DO want to know is how many lives are changed or saved because of the training those 12 volunteers have. Talking about the impact and the return on investment for your work is key to providing a powerful presentation.

Share the human impact by telling a story or two about your work.

Humanizing the work you do can turn a passive listener into an excited, willing funder. Telling how little Sonia, age 4, received medical care quickly for her broken arm so her mom only had to take a half day off work is much more powerful than saying "our clinic helps families deal with medical emergencies."

The real message in all of this is: Be comfortable with what you have to say and the best way to be comfortable is **to practice.**

Ask a colleague or family member to listen to your "pitch" and give you honest feedback. Have them tell you the truth about whether or not their minds wandered or if you were compelling.

An easy checklist to follow when sitting in front of funding panel:

- Be authentic.
- Listen to their questions.
- Speak clearly about the impact of your work.
- Remember to ask for the gift!

Originally posted January 19, 2011

Freshen Up

7 questions to ask to keep things fresh & exciting

I was watching an interview with U2's Bono recently about his success. He and his band have been touring and creating music for 30 years. It's not easy to sustain rock-stardom for such a very long-time.

What Bono said had me thinking about our sector and how we really don't focus on a simple tenet of success very well. He said **"keeping things fresh"** is a core reason for U2's success.

U2 doesn't just do the same thing over and over again because it's safe and has worked in the past. They don't simply repeat the same formula for writing songs or giving concerts. They take risks and keep things interesting, exciting and fresh.

Here are some ways U2 keeps things fresh:

- They find new and exciting venues for their performances.

- They communicate using multiple forms of social media as it has become an effective way to build community.
- They continue to look for ways to keep their work [their music & performances] fresh by digging down deep into themselves to tell stories that will touch others.
- They listen to what their fans are saying and provide what fans want at a level that is even better than last time.
- They take risks that excite themselves and their fans.

If you take a look at this list, which of these can you take on this year to keep the volunteer and donor experience at your organization fresh, rewarding, and creating more action/participation?

What I know for sure is that it takes time, thoughtful planning, and a focus on the volunteer or donor to keep things fresh. If you only focus on meeting your numbers and staying safe things get stale and people move on.

Seven questions to ask to keep things fresh:

1. Do we thank donors in ways that are meaningful to THEM?
2. Do we change the wording on the thank you letters regularly?
3. Do we have the board and long-time donors make thank you calls in the acknowledgment process?
4. Do we tell new, poignant and interesting stories everywhere? Online. In print. At in-person meetings?

5. Do we listen to our supporters to find out what excites them and to learn what MORE they'd like to know or experience about our work?

6. Are we sharing information monthly about the current financial status or what I call the "funding gap" so supporters are aware that there is more work to do?

7. Are our meetings & events edgy, engaging, informative, and cause people to WANT to support us more deeply?

Asking these seven questions can do a lot to move your organization and yourself out of the comfort zone.

Originally posted January 26, 2011

Staying Sane with Social Media

Excerpts from Minnesota Council of Nonprofits Technology Conference

Today Nicole Harrison (@SocialNicole) and I are delivering a fun breakout session at the Minnesota Council of Nonprofits Technology Conference: eSTRATEGY in an iWorld.

Our goal today is to calm some of the fears for nonprofit organizations wanting to use social media but really aren't sure where to begin.

Some key points from our session:

1. **It's SOCIAL.** Meaning you have interactions with others. You listen. They listen. You share. They share. There is a "talking" sure. But more important there is a listening. The place to start in social media is to listen. Listen to where your community is connecting. What are they saying? Who is doing the talking? What

can you learn from how, when and how often they are communicating?

2. It's about community, find it build it, add value to it.

3. Once you know where your community is hanging out. Hang with them and start communicating. I can't say enough how important it is to provide value with whatever avenue of social media you choose to use.

- Share startling statistics about the population you serve.
- Share stories that are compelling but dispel myths.
- Share links to other websites and information.
- Add value for your listeners every time you send a Tweet or post on LinkedIn, YouTube or Facebook.

4. It involves time and trust. You take time each day to eat, spend some quality moments with your family. . . why wouldn't you also spend time connecting with your community in ways that more deeply engage them? You don't have to do it all yourself either. Staff, volunteers, and donors are all a part of the community to engage and assist you with adding value to others.

5. It's not if you're going to play, but when. If you think social media is a fad or it's only for a younger generation, think again. It's here to stay. When my 70+ year-old mother got a Facebook page I knew there was no turning back. It's everywhere, this social media phenomenon. It's a powerful energy your organization can harness to get your community excited, enlightened, and even more deeply engaged.

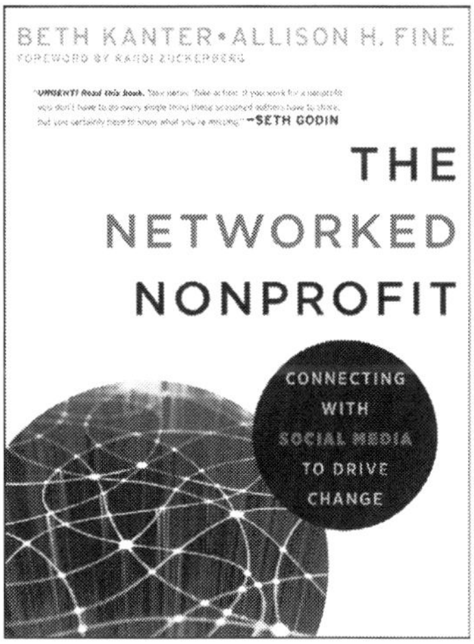

As Seth Godin, bestselling author & marketing guru says:

> *"How can you squander even one more day not taking advantage of the greatest shifts of our generation? How dare you settle for less when the world has made it so easy for you to be remarkable?"*

Yes, you want to have a social media policy and strategy. There are resources out there to help with both. The Mayo Clinic has their policy online so you can review it, print it, and use it as a template.

Don't let the creation of the policy or strategy bog you down. It's a great place to start engaging your community to help you create those for you.

Main message of today's session:
Get started. Listen for a bit. And then start providing value to your community. Have fun while you are doing it and above all, involve others in your community so it doesn't take all of YOUR time.

A must read for all organizations jumping into the social media revolution: *The Networked Nonprofit: Connecting with Social Media to Drive Change.*

Originally posted February 23, 2011

The Art of Asking

Last weekend I was honored to deliver multiple breakout sessions at the Habitat for Humanity Minnesota statewide conference. Amazing, hardworking volunteers and staff gathered for a couple of days to learn how to be better at all they do.

One of the sessions I delivered was The Art of Asking.

My session was geared to transform the fears and skepticism around asking. You can see the slides from the session at the bottom of this post.

A main theme of my work with social profit organizations comes from colleague and friend Lynne Twist. Lynne says: "Money moves toward boldness and clarity of communication."

I believe good fundraisers get a "yes" often. Exceptional fundraisers don't have to ask. Their communication is so compelling, engaging, and inviting that others want to take action. It's bold and clear communication that causes people to take action.

While our session last weekend was about asking, we also talked about generating support without having to ask. Read on for an example of generating support without asking. Has this ever happened at your organization? It can.

George, the CEO of an organization that must raise nearly $1.6 million in unrestricted funds each year from individuals in his community was attending a community event at the end of last year. The fiscal year for his organization was nearly at its end. It was December 22. George spoke at an event with 50 or so people from the community and told them the main things I coach organizations to touch on in ALL their face-to-face communication:

1. **What's working?** Share some good news or a story that is an example of great outcomes from a program.
2. **What's missing?** Share the current funding gap for a specific program and/or the agency overall. Share information about how many are on the waiting list for your services and what it would cost to provide support to them.
3. **Tell a story that causes people to feel something and want to take action.**

George shared a story a school age child, Tony. He described how twelve-year-old Tony's life is immensely better because of their afterschool program rather than being on the streets making choices he may regret and that would change the trajectory of his life forever.

The story was warm, had some humor, and it was enough for people to feel a bit of worry when George shared how the afterschool program would end the year the following week on December 31 with a $32,000 funding shortfall. George explained: “We still have a funding gap for Tony’s program despite our best efforts.”

George ended his 15-minute talk and moved on through the Christmas holiday. The following week, on December 30 he opened his mail to find a small note card from a woman who had attended the event the previous week. The note said: “I hope this helps Tony and the funding gap in the afterschool program.” Included with the note card was a check for $32,000. The funding gap for the afterschool program had just been eliminated! This gift was from someone who had never made a gift at that level before. A complete year-end surprise.

There had been no ask at the event where George spoke. He simply shared some facts. Shared from his heart and thanked the people in the room for all they’ve done throughout the year to support his agency.

The art of not asking.

Now I know there are times when it’s important to make the “ask” and invite a financial gift to support your organization. But I also remind you that there are lots of times throughout the year when asking is not yet appropriate; times when keeping your stakeholder community informed has as much or more value. The information you share in between the “asks” can and will often cause people to do more.

Here is a simple framework for communication that generates $ or support. Print, web, and in-person communication should answer these questions:

- What's your current funding gap?
- What would your organization do with more money or members? Humanize this.
- What is one simple action you want people to take? (Read the story? Attend an event? Tell others about you? Give something?)

And finally communication that generates support with ease should:

- Cause people to feel something.
- Unfold all year long. Communicate regularly.

Oh and by the way, George has shared with me numerous stories of how he shares the funding gap and compelling stories and often walks away with a check. He's really mastered the art of asking, or, not asking.

Originally posted March 16, 2011

Sawubona -- I See You

How well do you see your donors and volunteers?

Over a year ago, at a Minnesota Business Reputations event I was very excited to hear Chris Brogan (@ChrisBrogan) speak about building trust. The focus of Chris' interesting, edgy talk was about building trust online through the use of social media. I learned some new things about the importance of providing value, humanizing communication, and building loyal followers; all good things in both social media and in fundraising.

Chris used a greeting that cold February day that struck me deeply. I've used it over and over again in my fundraising trainings about building meaningful donor relationships.

Chris greeted the crowd with the word: **Sawubona. The Zulu greeting for "I see you."**

Think about it for just a moment. How meaningful to greet someone by telling them you see them? Wow. Don't we all just want to be seen for who we are, for just a moment?

As you wander through your fundraising year this year, **I challenge you and your organization to really "see" your supporters.** Your investors. Those who have given bits of themselves in support of furthering your mission and to helping others.

Unfortunately, this example I have of being seen is likely the norm and it didn't feel very good:

In the summer of 2009 I made a contribution of $400 to fund the garden for a childcare program at a large social profit organization. That's a pretty generous contribution for me and this was a new gift to a client I'd done some work with. They "heard" me when I shared that kids are the thing that can cause me to give. So their "ask" for a gift of $400 to fund the garden for kids under the age of five resonated with me and I said yes.

The summer passed. I may have received the perfunctory thank you letter for the gift, I don't recall. The fall came and went. And then I forgot about the contribution.

Fast-forward to December 2010. Over a year and a half later I received a Dear Friends letter from the organization asking me to consider increasing my gift from the previous year. As I read the letter my jaw dropped open.

I teach ***"fundraising is deep, profound relatedness"*** and I wasn't feeling very connected or related to them at that point. In fact, I was feeling a little like an ATM. They assumed that since I'd given once, I was likely to give again. I kept the letter to remind me to tell this story and to remind others how simple it would have been to "see" me and ensure another gift.

1. They could have sent a photo of the garden in full bloom.
2. They could have sent a photo of the garden with the KIDS in it.
3. They could have invited me to visit the garden.
4. The kids could have sent me an invitation to see the garden.
5. They could have sent a thank you from the kids – A messy, crayon-drawn thank you that let me know the garden was something that made a difference for those kids that summer.

Here are a few other ways to personalize your connection to your supporters. (These options are made quite simple with a good database that you've kept current noting donor interests and recent contacts.)

- When sending emails or letters make sure they are personalized. "Dear Lori" is a much more personal way to "see" someone than Dear Friends.
- Send updates throughout the year to segments of supporters with similar interests. e.g. Updates about how and what the kids are doing with the vegetables or flowers from the garden; or updates about the meals-on-wheels program to those who have a connection to seniors.

- Once or twice a year engage board members or other donors to make personal know-thy-donor calls to people who have given gifts of a certain size and above. Make sure the callers really listen to why the donor gave and learn something new about them.

- Only ask for money again after you've shared at least once how the previous gift was used and the impact it had.

- There are many, many more ways to personalize the connection a supporter has to your organization that doesn't take much time. What does your organization do to "see" your supporters?

Sawubona.

Originally posted March 30, 2011

Reflections on Receiving

Lessons from my bout with cancer

I've taken the last few weeks off to deal with health issues. It's not often I am removed from the day-to-day goings on of my business. I'm a work junkie. I love, love, love what I do. I get to hear the good news about how incredible people are doing incredible work across the country. And sometimes I get to help them do their work a little better.

Over the years I've taken for granted that the people being served by nonprofits would gladly welcome and accept the support, advice, food, clothes, or whatever the nonprofit organization was giving them. Why wouldn't they? People were just wanting to help them, right?

Then I was diagnosed with cancer. And found I had to accept

support, advice, food, and love from my community. It was uncomfortable, scary and something I realized I wasn't very good at.

Here's the quick recap:
In January I found a lump in my breast. In February I was diagnosed with breast cancer and the treatment was a unilateral mastectomy. I chose April 1 on purpose to keep my sense of humor about it all and to make sure to get all my clients "taken care of" before I took any time off.

While doing the mastectomy my surgeon also removed a small mole from my stomach. . . that turned out to be melanoma. A week later I had additional surgery to remove all the "margins" around it so it wouldn't spread. Two types of cancer in two weeks. . . yikes.

Throughout the past few months I've shared my news as necessary with family, friends, colleagues, and clients. I didn't make a big huge announcement, as I was certain this was a minor thing I would and could handle easily. Fortunately, much of that is true. Though I've had some complications and had yet a third and fourth surgery in April to put all of this behind me, the fantastic news is no chemo and no radiation. Whew!

What happened to me as I shared my news was a deeper respect for clients of the many organizations I work with. I instantly had an "insiders" view about what it's like to feel helpless, needy, and way too much of a burden to my inner circle than I've ever wanted to be. And I think of myself as a pretty strong, self-sufficient woman.

What must it be like for the Dad of two daughters who loses his job then can't pay rent and becomes homeless? How does he accept help and still feel good about himself? Or the Mom who works two jobs but doesn't have health insurance with either job so when her six-year-old son cuts his leg and needs stitches she has to find somewhere to provide free or low-cost medical care?

How must they feel? For me, although I've been grateful for the support, care, and prayers, I've felt like a burden at times, ashamed that I got sick, and often incredibly uncomfortable with the support lovingly given to me.

So I vowed to use this experience to remind myself and the caregivers and volunteers at the organizations doing good work why their clients might show up with anger, frustration, fear, embarrassment, or shame.

Maybe you already know and understand, but just in case you don't, please know **not everyone finds it easy to "accept" and "receive." We, many of us who were taught to take care of ourselves, feel it's a sign of weakness to accept help from others.** We get angry and embarrassed that we can't drive ourselves to a doctor appointment or pick up our own prescription or make dinner because we are too tired. We want to hide but can't because we need our community to get through the crisis.

That said, I humbly thank my fundraising community colleagues who have been generously submitting guest posts for me during this time of healing and recovery.

I'm still healing. Four surgeries in two weeks takes a toll on a person AND her family, I might add. But I believe I'll come out the other side of this adventure a calmer, more compassionate, and more peaceful person.

Once I'm back up to full-strength the buildings I'll leap may be a few stories shorter but I'll still wear my cape and expect fundraising miracles. And now I'll be watching to make sure those being served also receive warm hugs and hand squeezes when I see fear or uncertainty in their eyes.

I hope you will too.

Originally posted April 20, 2011

Little Things Add Up to Something Big

Ensure engagement by paying attention to details

Often I'm asked to work with the staff and board of a social profit organization to help create an annual fundraising plan or better define their funding gap message or the board and staff relationship.

When I begin work with these organizations I often find that what I'm REALLY being brought in for is to help ease frustration. The staff has grown frustrated with the board or key volunteers who are not taking action in the way the staff wants.

The board or key volunteers, while passionate about the work of the organization, don't quite know what action to take, which sometimes results in them being "checked out."

In my careful observation of their work and communication I often see the same issues over and over. I believe most of these frustrations can be eliminated with more specific communication that focuses on the details of each goal and measures for success as they relate to real people.

Here are a few actions that focus on those details that can make a huge difference:

PASSION RE-TREAD

Staff:

Create the ability for all board members to see your mission in action and to learn a story of a client by actually meeting someone your organization serves.

Volunteer Leadership:

Hunger for the connection to clients & the mission. Routinely have one board member tell a story of a real person (client) at each board meeting. Hold board meetings in different locations where you can be connected to the special people served by your organization.

GOALS & ACTION ITEMS

Staff:

Take GREAT meeting notes. Highlight goals and actions. Always list the person accountable and a "by when" date of accomplishing the action. Spend less time on notes that are a "he said, she said" recap. Provide your powerful, action-focused notes quickly following all committee and board meetings (within 2 days).

Volunteer Leadership:

READ the notes. Do what you said you'd do, by when you said you'd do it. If the timing doesn't work contact the appropriate staff and "re-promise" with a date that works for you. These are your goals. Take action on them.

MEASURES & ACCOUNTABILITY

Staff:

Provide reports that clearly show goals and team activity. These can be charts, bar graphs, or whatever visual display best shows the progress (or lack thereof) being made on the agreed on goals. These should be provided to the volunteer leadership so that a "peer to peer" discussion on progress can take place.

Volunteer Leadership:

Request the charts and details about agreed on actions (e.g. making thank you calls to all donors $200+). Read the reports at board or committee meetings and discuss YOUR own activity regularly. Use the data to discuss what is working with the goals and actions and what needs more attention or discussion

GOVERNANCE

Staff:

Work with board leadership to clearly define accountabilities with an annual board agreement. Also identify and provide structure for very clear goals for new board member identification, recruitment and orientation.

Volunteer Leadership:

Within the board or your committee pay attention to who is doing what. Are all board members or committee members providing value? Showing up at meetings? Does everyone know what is expected with regard to board involvement, especially with regard to fundraising? not, invite help, guidance, and input from the staff and others outsider your group to put together a framework of participation. Seek to ensure every board member and community volunteer feels like a helping hero and has a clear picture of what is expected.

Each of these areas deserves much more time than I'm devoting here. Suffice it to say, attention to the communication between staff, board, and community volunteers is critical.

The fundraising action planning sessions and other workshops I deliver allow you an opportunity to delve more deeply into each of these topics. And, you can certainly tackle these areas yourselves.

Recipe for success: Awareness and clear, authentic, honoring communication about the small, but powerful details.

Originally posted May 18, 2011

The Soul of Money

A book that changed my life

I've read the amazing book *The Soul of Money: Reclaiming the Wealth of Our Inner Resources* by colleague and friend, Lynne Twist, countless times and I've purchased more than 100 copies to give as a gift to nonprofit staffs, boards, and philanthropists.

Through its beautiful stories and poignant personal examples *The Soul of Money* takes us through a thorough and critical look at how we've given our power over to money. Lynne asks us to take a deep look at our relationship with money as development professionals, parents, business owners, employees, and engaged community members, to identify the true purpose of money for each of us and how it connects with our own core values.

Lynne believes, as I do, **that our work in the social profit sector is sacred work.**

In chapter five: **Money is like Water** we learn the story of Gertrude, a woman most people would call poor. This chapter provides a true example of the power of money when it is infused with purpose, integrity, and aligned with our soul.

On her way from San Francisco to Harlem, New York, Lynne stopped in Chicago to visit with the CEO of a major corporation to pick up a large check for The Hunger Project, the organization where she was working as a fundraiser.

Lynne had been told that the major food corporation based in the tall, glass high-rise was guilty of some business practices that were a bit nasty and had an image problem. The corporation believed that by making a significant contribution to The Hunger Project they could start to clean up their image.

The stop to pick up the check was scheduled for the morning of the visit to Harlem. Lynne made her way to the CEO's large office where he sat with his head down, back-lit by the sun shining through the large picture window. She could barely see his face during the meeting as he pushed the check across the desk. He clearly wanted her gone quickly. As Lynne describes it, "I felt the guilt of the company coming right across that desk with the money." (p. 99)

After the awkward meeting, Lynne hurried to the airport and made her way to New York City where she had been invited to visit. The feeling of the company's shame stayed with Lynne through the plane ride and car ride to Harlem.

Lynne arrived in the midst of a rainstorm for the meeting located in the basement of an old church building in Harlem. She was late due to the weather, and entered the room packed with people who had heard about the work of The Hunger Project. They had waited patiently for Lynne's arrival while buckets collected the rain dripping into the basement; a world apart from the gleaming bright CEO office from earlier in the day.

Lynne made her presentation with warmth and engaging stories and then came to the part where it was time to "ask for the money." Though the room was full of the "working poor" Lynne made her request and then waited quietly.

After a few seconds of silence, a woman near the back stood up. She was in her late 60s or early 70s with graying hair and wrinkled hands and face. She stood tall, erect, and proud and said:

> *"Girl, my name is Gertrude and I like what you've said and I like you. Now I ain't got no checkbook or credit cards. To me, money is a lot like water. For some folks it rushes through their lives like a raging river. Money comes through my life like a little trickle. But I want to pass it on in a way that does the most good for the most folks. I see it as my right and my responsibility. It's also my joy. I have fifty dollars in my purse that I earned from doing a white woman's wash and I want to give it to you."*

Gertrude walked up the aisle and handed Lynne her $50 cash and then many others followed. On the plane ride back to San Francisco Lynne realized that below the ones and fives in her briefcase from the folks in Harlem was the $50,000 check from the food company.

The difference was the money from Gertrude and her friends carried the energy of commitment to make a difference. And right then, even knowing that The Hunger Project desperately needed the funding, Lynne decided to return the check to the CEO.

Fast-forward five or six years after the $50,000 contribution was returned. Lynne received a letter from the CEO. He had since retired and had received a very lucrative exit package for his work. In his letter he shared how the return of the $50,000 was one of the most significant memories of his career. He had enclosed a check for many times the original amount and made it clear that he wanted the money to make a difference. He wanted to make a meaningful contribution to end world hunger.

I believe it is our job as development professionals to "invite the money to stop by" to make its impact before it moves on to the next place. And when we invite financial support that is a true expression of who a person truly is, it is a gift to the giver and to the organization.

The book is an awesome read. I hope you'll give the gift to yourself to enjoy the wisdom from *The Soul of Money*.

Originally posted May 25, 2011

Fund Development Committees -- What Do They Do Anyway?

Key responsibilities for successful fund development committees

Here's a question I often get asked: "What makes an effective fund development committee? What are ways people can contribute effectively even if they don't have big money connections, etc.?"

Carter McNamara answered this really well earlier this year in his blog, but I'd like to add to his post. From Carter:

> *"One of the biggest misconceptions about the Fundraising Committee is that its members are to do the fundraising for the nonprofit. No, the job of the Fundraising Committee is to ensure that the fundraising is done very well. The actual fundraising should be done by all Board members, with various staff members supporting those Board members."*

I agree with Carter, the full board should be involved with the fund development process at an organization. Just a reminder though: Fund Development is, as defined by the Association of Fundraising Professionals: "The total process by which an organization increases public understanding of its mission and acquires financial support for its programs."

In my fundraising action planning sessions we work to identify three or four strategic fundraising goals for the organization that include ways for the entire staff and board to participate in development. This is a key to success for any organization. Simple ways for all staff and board to be involved can mean:

- Telling powerful compelling client stories
- Sharing the funding gap with the community so people know what's needed (this is different from asking for money)
- Inviting guests e.g. donors or prospects to upcoming events
- Thanking recent donors via phone call and/or personal notes
- Or simply inviting guests (donors) to "business as usual" events like graduations or the school play or a volunteer training

In addition to my short list of development activities here are Carter's six primary responsibilities for the fundraising or development committee:

1. **Ensure there's a specific fundraising target:** How much money needs to be raised? Usually the amount is the difference between expected revenues and expenses. Usually those revenues and expenses are identified during strategic or program planning.

2. **Ensure prospect research occurs to identify how much money might be raised from different types of resources:** Good prospect research will look at the nature of the nonprofit's services and its lo-

cale, and identify similar nonprofits and the sources of funding used by them. Good prospect research will go beyond searching a database of foundations to submit proposals to.

3. **Identify specific, potential sources of funds from a diverse mix of sources:** Now the nonprofit is ready to start selecting specific sources of funds from individuals, foundations, government and/or fees. These activities should result in the names of specific sources, for example, names of people, foundations and government agencies, and/or the specific amounts of fees to charge for certain services.

4. **Develop an action plan about who is going to approach what source, how and by when*:** This responsibility includes identifying which Board members will approach what source, along with what staff members will support those Board members. All Board members should have assignments, not just the members of the Fundraising Committee. (*Note from Lori: This does not mean all board members must ask for money. It does mean board members can accompany staff on asks and share why they serve on the board and examples of client stories that may inspire the prospect.)

5. **Compile the results of items 1- 4 into a Fundraising Plan that is approved by the Board:** The Plan should include more than merely a listing of what foundations to approach. The Plan becomes the roadmap for generating sufficient revenue. It should include realistic expectations from a diversity of sources, and justify how those sources were identified. It should

include an action plan (from step 4) that the Fundraising Committee ensures is implemented on a timely basis.

6. **Ensure effective administrative systems to track grants and donations:** As funding comes into the nonprofit, its various sources and amounts must be closely and accurately documented. Acknowledgements and receipts must be provided back to donors. Grant requirements must be monitored to ensure they are met. In the United States, fundraising information must be included on the IRS Form 990.

Summary – Job of the Fundraising Committee is to Ensure Planful, Strategic Fundraising.

Originally posted Wednesday, July 20, 2011

Talking About Money So People Want to Give

Sharing the funding gap

Quickly, can you share with me where your organization is right now in meeting your annual fundraising goals? Does your board chair, CEO, and do YOU know what the current funding gap is for your organization? How often do you share those money details with your community?

I define the funding gap as the amount of money you have to raise from the community each year: OR the difference between the annual budget and the sources of funding you can absolutely count on, like grants, that you've already been approved for, United Way support, gov't funding, fees for service, etc.

Why share this information regularly? If your community isn't certain you need more of their time, dollars, advice, contacts, whatever it is that is missing – they may in fact, go elsewhere.

As marketing guru and author Seth Godin says, "nonprofits sell feeling good."

Your supporter community wants to feel like they are helping you do something you could not do without them. But the key here is: They have to KNOW what it is you want them to do.

CEOs who shy away from talking about the money, the funding gap, and that there is much more to do, are often stuck on the feeling that talking about what you need more of will cause people to think the organization is not run well. I believe the exact opposite. When you are transparent about costs, goals, and the impact of a gift, you build a stronger and more committed supporter community. Sharing this information though, can't be boring and full of charts and graphs. It has to be shared with examples of compelling stories about real people.

In my ebook Nine Steps to Successful Fundraising Campaigns, step # 7 is to keep the money conversation visible: in print, on your website, via multiple forms of communication to allow transparency and encourage widespread participation.

When you keep all eyes on the goal, OTHERS will help you reach it.

I recommend organizations, especially the CEO, share the progress on their annual fundraising goals, i.e. the funding gap, often, in fun, interesting ways throughout the year. Don't wait until the final days of the year to scurry and beg for support.

Breaking your annual goal into smaller, bite-size "mini-campaigns" can also make it easier for supporters to want to take action and possibly make more than one contribution a year. What does it cost per seat for your organization to put on a wonderful theater or music performance? Share that. Or what does it cost per child to ensure they are going to graduate from high school and venture out into the world prepared for college or their first job? Share that.

Humanize the funding gap with stories of real people who will be impacted by meeting or not meeting your goal.

Compel your supporters with the impact of what you CAN do more of to help real people AND share where you are at in the race to reach your goals. I promise this sort of clear communication will generate surprising results.

Originally posted Wednesday, August 31, 2011

Before You Begin Drafting Your Year-End Appeal

The importance of the right database

It's that time of year again. Kids have returned to school, the pace has quickened for getting things done, and it's time to start thinking about your year-end fundraising appeals. But before you get too far, I encourage you to make sure your database is in tiptop shape and ready to go.

I believe your donor data is like money in the bank. A well maintained, up-to-date data tracking system can mean the difference between meeting your financial goals and missing them.

We often talk about databases in terms of what sort of information is stored, how often it's updated, and how it's maintained, but your database is also more than that, it's also the software used to store the institutional memory of your organization. It's the collective wisdom gathered and hopefully easily accessed when you need to learn more about what to do next. With something so vital to accomplishing your mission and your fundraising goals, it's critical that you have the exact right fit and your system does all that you want it to.

Do you love the donor management system you're using? Does it have all the functionality you need? Can you and others on your team easily enter and retrieve information?

If you answered NO to any of my questions you may want to take a look at what else is out there. "The Consumer's Guide to Low Cost Donor Management Systems" is a great resource.

I'm very proud to say that the contact management system I use and recommend, Trail Blazer, was included as one of the Top 10 systems that "offer the best combination of functionality, price, and attractiveness in a variety of situations."

I actually had a tiny role in helping to create the nonprofit version of Trail Blazer's software. What I like is that your team is not limited to purchasing "modules" – you get the "whole enchilada" for one annual fee. And, there is no limit or different price for more than one user or for any of the awesome training & support the team provides. Once you've evaluated your database, both the information it contains and the software used to run it, and you're ready to plan your year-end fundraising appeal – NOW you have to draft it. Good luck!

Originally posted Wednesday, September 14, 2011

Ending the Nonprofit Starvation Cycle

With an excerpt from Standford Social Innovation Review

It's the time of year where I'm helping lots of organizations draft their annual fall appeal letters and I've been bumping into conversations with some of them about how to tell donors about administrative costs v. program costs.

My first recommendation is: **Don't go there.**
My second recommendation is: **Before you mention anything about those costs have you:**

1. Shared real life examples of the human impact of your programs? Like a name, age, and real example of a real person.
2. Made sure to explain to your supporters that there are people on waiting lists or programs are filled to the seams?
3. Shared your annual funding gap so supporters

understand there is more to do with the unrestricted fundraising dollars you are raising?

4. Shared real examples about the quality of staff and systems necessary to deliver your life-changing and life-saving programs?

My third recommendation AFTER you've done all of the above is: Read the article from Stanford Social Innovation: "The Nonprofit Starvation Cycle." Here's an excerpt:

The Nonprofit Starvation Cycle

> *"A vicious cycle is leaving nonprofits so hungry for decent infrastructure that they can barely function as organizations – let alone serve their beneficiaries. The cycle starts with funders' unrealistic expectations about how much running a nonprofit costs, and results in nonprofits misrepresenting their costs while skimping on vital systems – acts that feed funders' skewed beliefs. To break the nonprofit starvation cycle, funders must take the lead."*

I believe it's our duty as nonprofit leadership to educate our funders, including our individual donors about the real costs of running our organizations. Paying attention to quality IT systems, staff salaries and benefits, as well as rent, utilities, and so on, are all part of the necessary ingredients to delivering quality programs. Somehow we've been trained to think we should deliver world-class services with less than world-class infrastructure, staff, and essential overhead expenditures.

So, I strongly suggest that rather than talking about how lean your organization is and the low overhead/expense ratio, talk about the impact of your work on one life, one family and keep us focused on the reason you need unrestricted overhead in the first place.

I find that donors writing checks want to know their dollars will be well spent and real people will be helped. When it's explained to them that there are costs associated with doing quality work they understand the ratio of expenses might be higher than they've been trained to pay attention to.

It's an opportunity we ALL have as we invite financial support this fall.

Originally posted Wednesday, October 12, 2011

Donors Ask the Wrong Question

Notes from Dan Pallotta's keynote speech

Last week I attended the Social Venture Partners International conference in Minneapolis. I've been an associate partner at SVP since 2006 and this was my first international conference. On Friday morning our keynote speaker was the amazing Dan Pallotta, a leading expert on innovation in the nonprofit sector. His book *Uncharitable: How Restraints on Nonprofits Undermine Their Potential* is a must read.

So as a follow-up to last week's post: "Ending the Nonprofit Starvation Cycle," which talked about administrative overhead and the question most often asked of a charity: What is your administrative overhead? The myth and assumption is that lower is better. In the previ I made a mild attempt to dispel this myth but Dan takes the topic full on. Here's some of what he had to say:

Dan's observation is that we have two rulebooks: One for charity and one for the rest of the economic world. We blame capitalism for creating huge inequities in our society. . . and we refuse to allow the nonprofit sector to actually use the tools of capitalism to rectify those inequities.

He took us through 5 areas where the rulebook of discrimination plays out:

1. **Compensation:** In the for-profit sector we allow the payment of a competitive wage based on the value people produce, but we don't like to see people make a lot of money in the nonprofit sector. We have a very visceral reaction to the notion that anyone would make a lot of money helping other people. But we have no similar visceral reaction when people make a lot of money NOT helping others or even hurting others.

2. **Advertising & Marketing:** We give the for-profit sector huge latitude to spend spend spend and find new customers until the last dollar no longer produces a penny of value. We don't like to see donations spent on advertising in charity. Our attitude is if you can get the advertising for free or donated, I'm fine with that. But I don't want you spending my donation on advertising because I want my money to go to the needy. As if the money spent on advertising couldn't potentially and dramatically enlarge the amount of money going to the needy.

John Kenneth Galbraith, the Canadian American economist said, "The for-profit sector creates desires. It creates wants that you didn't know you had. First it creates the product and then through the massive engines of marketing and advertising it creates the market for that product. But we are supposed to create a market for philanthropy to end hunger and disease and everything else without actually spending any money."

3. **Risk taking for new donors:** Specifically in pursuit of new donors and the area of fundraising. We are not talking about taking programmatic risks to figure out a new way to mentor teen gang members or build wells in Africa. Here again the for-profit sector gets every advantage. Paramount Pictures can make a $150 million movie that flops and no one calls the attorney general. It's considered part of their business model to make a lot of movies. Some of them succeed and some of them fail. More succeed than fail. And on that basis they build huge empires.

4. So nonprofit organizations are petrified of trying any bold, risky, really high profile community fundraising endeavors for fear that if the thing fails that will be the end of them. Meanwhile Hollywood, every week is placing $150 million bets on ridiculous movie ideas.

5. **Time horizon – the time it takes to get a return on investment to our donors:** Amazon is a great example. They went for six years without any return to investors because everyone understood there was a long-term objective called building market dominance at the end of the line. If some charity ever had an incredi-

ble vision of building scale that required that for six years no money was going to go to the needy we'd expect a crucifixion.

6. Profit: The for-profit sector can pay people in order to attract their capital. The nonprofit sector by definition cannot. So the for-profit sector monopolizes the multi-trillion dollar capital markets; the nonprofit sector is starved for growth capital and risk capital.

You put these five things together: You can't use money to lure talent; you can't advertise on the scale the for-profit sector can; you cannot take the kinds of risks in pursuit of new customers; you don't have the same amount of time to find those customers; and you don't have the stock market. So we put the nonprofit sector at the most unbelievably extreme disadvantage on every level. . . and we call the whole system charity.

There are 3 main problems with the overhead question:

- Makes us think overhead is not part of the cause -- the important work being done.
- Forces charities to go without the things they really need to solve the problem.
- Gives donors bad information.

The most memorable line from Dan was: **Fundraising builds capacity to build capacity.** What I took away from Dan's remarks: Our job is to change the status quo. Ask different questions. If, indeed, we want to end hunger or homelessness are we willing to level or change the playing field and give nonprofits the resources to get the job done? Are we?

Wednesday, October 19, 2011

You Can't Thank Them Too Much

Musing on donor acknowledgements

As a follow up to my enewsletter from last week I want to step a bit deeper into the donor thank you theme. It's a busy time of year for nonprofits in generating gifts and I am often underwhelmed at the sorry state of affairs when it comes to acknowledging gifts.

Here are some examples of good, bad, and ugly acknowledgment from both the non and for-profit world:

The Good

- Thursday, Nov. 3, I received a warm thank you call due to an online gift made on Tuesday, Nov. 1. The CEO and I chatted for a few minutes. I was reminded why I admire their work and felt great about my contribution. Total time invested by the organization: 5 minutes.
- My spouse received a warm thank you letter after having some email interaction with Pandora about the

security of their website. Actually signed with a pen... not sure it was by Tim, the CEO, but the letter made Mark feel great about his experience. The letter was sent within a day or two of the email exchange. Timely, warm, and created good feelings.

- I received a follow-up call last week from Sara at Minnesota Public Radio for the online fall contribution I had just made. She was phoning to make sure they had recorded the gift correctly since they were having website processing issues the day I made the gift. Timely and thorough follow-up.

The Bad

- My spouse and I are still waiting for the "official" thank you call or letter from an organization that normally does immediate follow-up after they receive contributions. We love the thank you calls as much as attending their event because we get a chance to connect with people we admire to tell them we appreciate their work. It's been nearly three weeks and they have already processed the credit card transaction. We've been wondering how we were forgotten and how many others were as well? What steps could they take to ensure great follow-up next time?

The Ugly

- I have received a third "Dear Friends" letter from an organization I gave a gift to in 2009. You can read more about that gift interaction in the "Sawubona" chapter on page 68. I had not heard from them for 18 months until December of 2010 when they sent the

> first Dear Friends letter asking me to increase my gift. There has been no other communication in that void of time between my first gift and the requests for subsequent gifts that causes me to have a good feeling about WHY I had a connection with them in the first place. I'm sad to say, their letters feel demanding and like I owe them something.

Suggestions from my enewsletter for thanking donors that will cause your organization to stand out:

1. First time donor thank you letters, say it right in the letter: Thank you for your first gift!

2. Donors who are making a 2nd or 3rd gift THIS YEAR: Be sure you let them know you notice their multiple gifts this year and are grateful.

3. Personal notes at the bottom of the thank you letter that are personalized to that donor are powerful.

4. And the most powerful way to thank: Short, warm thank you calls from a board member, client, or volunteer made within a few days of receiving the gift.

I'd love to hear your suggestions to creatively stay connected to your donors through acknowledgement practices?

Wednesday, November 09, 2011

This is Philanthropy

A couple days ago I had a colleague share a story of how she secured a $100,000 gift for her organization earlier this month. At the end of the story about "the ask," where she shared a few of the nuggets of how the prospect was engaged, how easy it was to talk with him, and how the time passed quickly, my friend Beverly paused and said those words with a gleam in her eye, "THIS is philanthropy."

She was talking about the ease and joy in the hour plus meeting that resulted in the donor feeling totally listened to, inspired by the project he was going to provide a first gift for, and for the way he felt about making the gift in memory of his recently deceased wife. **The meeting was filled with laughter, tears, photos, stories and NOT charts, graphs, and donor giving pyramids.**

The interesting thing about this exciting gift solicitation, and I hesitate to even call it a solicitation but really a "nudging of the inevitable," was that Beverly, the major gifts officer, had never met this donor before. She had her colleague, someone who knew the donor prospect well, set up the meeting and they did their prep work ahead of time to determine who would take what role in the meeting and fully fleshed out the important topics to cover.

There were no sweaty palms or fears that this was difficult. There WAS authentic talking and listening – which I believe is the true definition of communication.

Inviting financial support, when you've done your homework can, and should, feel like Beverly described. It should leave you and the donor with a glow of warmth about the good things that can happen because of the gift that was just promised.

The Art of Asking is no big secret. It is practice & planning, a bit of good research, with a dash of good timing and a whole bushel of good communication before, during, and after the "ask"; including the listening part of communication.

Kudos to Beverly for a job well done!

Wednesday, November 30, 2011

Are you ready to raise more funds than ever before?

Dear Heart-Centered Fundraiser,

If you have just finished reading this book I know you are passionate about your work. You may be looking for ways to share with your community the impact a financial gift has in changing or saving lives. I bet you often work long hours and worry if you are doing everything you can to raise all the dollars it takes to run your organization.

You want to do more, but are unsure how or what to do. Let me offer you a fresh perspective.

When you shift to look at what's working NOW with clients and donors, something inside you shifts. Focusing on what is working well and sharing messages about that, combined with messages about the impact of the money changes everything for your fundraising.

It's all about perspective. When you shift your perspective to one of possibility and taking action, your world changes and you feel inspired, hopeful, and powerful. But learning how to do so, through coaching, can be costly. That's where I come in.

My strategies & tools have helped organizations to collectively raise more than $150 million from individuals! Most of my clients met or exceeded their goals in the past several years. Even in this economy. I'm not telling you this to brag; rather, to let you know the tools I use are effective. I get results. Because I'm committed to ensuring success, I've had many, many requests for one-on-one coaching from fundraising professionals just like you. As much as I would love to help every person, I'm just not able to. While reflecting on this dilemma, I realized many organizations could benefit from coaching, but may not be able to afford an onsite coach.

IGNITED
ONLINE FUNDRAISING
COMMUNITY

It was up to me to find the solution, so I created the **Ignited Online Fundraising Community.** My goal is to provide you with monthly support and new tools that will recharge and reenergize you for the important work you do.

When you join the **Ignited Online Fundraising Community,** you receive:

- Master coaching sessions with me throughout the year
- Monthly, one-hour webinars with top national and international expert speakers focused on innovative possibilities
- Monthly email messages with helpful tips and links to articles, reports, and blogs pertinent to what is important to you
- And more!

If you're ready for ongoing access to the newest, most up-to-date strategies for delivering your message to donors who can't wait to support you, join me and the **Ignited Online Fundraising Community!**

Visit: http://www.lorijacobwith.com/membership/index.htm

51923477R00063

Made in the USA
Lexington, KY
10 May 2016